Questo libro appartiene a

~~Giulia~~

Luca

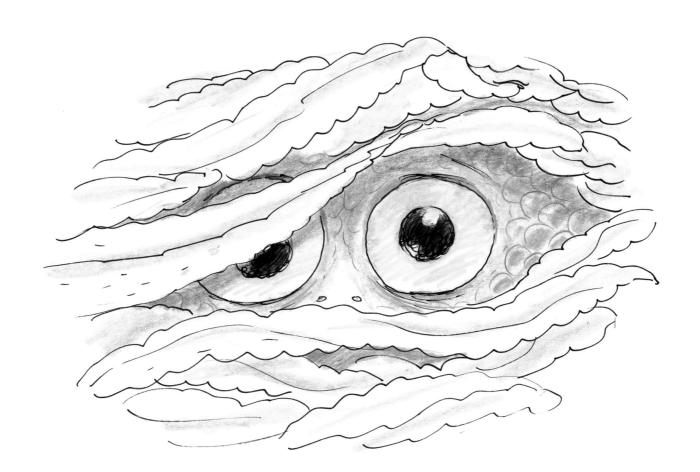

THE ART OF

Disney · PIXAR

LUCA

Foreword by Enrico Casarosa

Introduction by Daniela Strijleva

CHRONICLE BOOKS
SAN FRANCISCO

Library of Congress Cataloging-in-Publication Data is available.
ISBN 978-1-7972-0725-4
Manufactured in China.

Design by Liam Flanagan.

10 9 8 7 6 5 4 3 2 1

Chronicle Books LLC
680 Second Street
San Francisco, California 94107
www.chroniclebooks.com

Ape is a trademark of Piaggio & C. S.p.A.
Vespa is a trademark of Piaggio & C. S.p.A.
Piaggio is a trademark of Piaggio & C. S.p.A.

(front cover) Daniel López Muñoz, *pencil and digital paint*

(back cover) Daniel López Muñoz, *digital paint*

(front flap) McKenna Harris, *digital paint*

(back flap) Yon Hui Lee, *digital paint*

(endsheets) Josh Holtsclaw, *digital*

(page 1) Matthias De Clercq, *colored pencil and ink*

(previous spread) Ernesto Nemesio, *digital paint*

(above) Deanna Marsigliese, *ink and marker*

PORTOFINO

Daniela Strijleva, *ink and watercolor*

FOREWORD

Truth is, I wouldn't be writing this foreword had I not met my best friend, Alberto. I wouldn't have chased my dreams from Italy to the United States in my early twenties, and I wouldn't have found a career in animation.

We were both eleven when we met. I was shy and sheltered, and he was outspoken and gregarious—a largely unsupervised troublemaker. We hit it off right away. Alberto had a different interest every other week, and I was happy to follow him. One day he'd be building an aquarium, and the next he'd be skateboarding down steep hills, shooting off fireworks, or fishing off the cliffs. One time he bought a pet python and snuck it into school for several months. He confided years later that he was terribly afraid of it, but that he bought the snake to conquer his fear.

As it was, nothing ever got boring with Alberto. We were always exploring and running around the small medieval *caruggi* (narrow streets) of our hometown, Genova. But summers at the sea were what we loved the best. Genova is a seaport town in the middle of the Ligurian coast, also called the Italian Riviera. We spent our days taking trains to different beaches and rocky outcroppings along the coast. We shared some amazing food on these outings: *focaccia* and *farinata* (Ligurian flatbreads), *anguria* (watermelon), and tons of *gelati* and *ghiaccioli* (ice cream and ice pops)—flavors that to this day transport me right back to a rock by the sea. There weren't many sea cliffs that we didn't jump off, and Alberto was always there to dare me to leap. It was scary, thrilling, and freeing all at once.

Chances are you have that one special friend you grew up with whose passion, and sometimes questionable judgment, dragged you into some adventures—what today we'd call "growth opportunities." With this movie I wanted to celebrate the kind of deep friendships that help us uncover who we want to be, the friendships that usher us into adulthood and that we carry with us for the rest of our lives. I also wanted to celebrate those never-ending days in the sun filled with summer sensations and the intoxicating possibilities of what comes next.

Lastly, I'd be remiss not to talk about leaping from the highest cliff of all—namely, the epic journey of making this film. Once again, I was able to find the courage with friends by my side: the most talented and giving team I could ever have dreamed of. This book contains just a tiny fraction of the amazing and creative contributions from some of my friends and colleagues at Pixar.

I sincerely hope you enjoy it.

Enrico Casarosa, Director

PS: I have a favor to ask.... Reach out to that friend you once had from those formative days of awkward adolescence and self-discovery. It'll give you the opportunity to tell them how important they've been in your life. I bet they might even remember some hilarious moments you've long forgotten.

INTRODUCTION

Luca is a film that follows a special summer friendship, and a young boy who finds his place in the world because of it. We've all had that one summer of change that almost imperceptibly brought us closer to the outer edge of childhood—a summer full of friendship, adventure, and carefree days. *Luca* tells this story.

For our team of filmmakers, the process of finding the story was not unlike the process of growing up. At first there were just a few of us, creating scribbled drawings, analog paintings, notes on loose papers. Like a puzzle, the fragments produced by our collective imaginations were jumbled, waiting to be solved. We found our first answers in our director Enrico's early watercolors. They spoke with a strong sense of color, texture, history, charm, and childlike fun. It was an exciting start to an adventure that we would embark on together.

Luckily for us, collaborating with Enrico was easy. As an intuitively visual storyteller, one who effortlessly invites a dialogue with fellow artists centered around images, he made us feel at home in the creation of *Luca*. He also took us to his homeland, Italy, and guided us through the places of his own boyhood summers. We studied the narrow alleys of the Cinque Terre towns, savored *focaccia* and *trofie al pesto*, went on fishing expeditions, and swam in the azure Mediterranean waters.

Seated in the piazza, *gelato* in hand, we watched children splash into the blue, while fishermen regaled us with stories of the old ways of life. These moments transported us to our own childhoods—and from this place within ourselves, Luca's world began taking shape.

When we returned, our art reflected this deeper meaning. If classic Italian films, history books, and travel posters gave us the first curious tastes of 1950s Italy, the physical place awakened all our senses to the setting.

Equipped with this new perspective, we set about visually expressing Luca's strong emotional experiences in an equally bold way. We opted for a pure and saturated palette reminiscent of the Italian summer, the colors of the Cinque Terre, and the shiny 1950s Vespas. We exaggerated the details, because kids notice details in an exaggerated way. We turned to theater, puppetry, storybooks, and handcrafted folk art to inspire our set and character designs, while tirelessly researching and honoring the rich history and uniqueness of the Cinque Terre. In designing Portorosso, we tasked ourselves with capturing the slice-of-life feel of a small fishing town that seamlessly fit in with the rest of the Cinque Terre. To us, Portorosso was, and always will be, a very real place.

To craft this world, our artists have worked with passion and love for years. This book is, in turn, a love letter to them in gratitude for their giving of themselves, solving the puzzle, and collaborating to make the story of *Luca* come to life.

We now near the end of our filmmaking journey. Here we are, like Luca, forever changed by the friendships made, the bonds formed, and our own special summer creating the art of *Luca*.

Daniela Strijleva, Production Designer

Daniela Strijleva, *ink and watercolor*

(this page) Enrico Casarosa, *colored pencil and watercolor*

10

(this page) Daniela Strijleva, *watercolor and gouache*

(above) Daniela Strijleva, *ink and watercolor*

(right) Enrico Casarosa, *ink and watercolor*

12

Daniel López Muñoz, *pencil and digital paint*

(left) Don Shank, *colored pencil*

(below) Deanna Marsigliese,
ink and marker

(above) Deanna Marsigliese,
ink and marker

(above) Don Shank, *colored pencil*

(above) Deanna Marsigliese,
ink and marker

Luca has big, round eyes, the largest of all of the characters in our film. This is because Luca leads with his eyes. They illustrate how he experiences and engages with the world around him. He's open and curious, savoring every new discovery and taking everything in.

DEANNA MARSIGLIESE, Character Art Director

Don Shank, *colored pencil*

To stylize the sea monster scales in a handmade and storybook way, we drew our inspirations from paper models, fabric costumes, and sculptures. The scales are reflective in a handmade, faceted way.

JENNIFER CHIA-HAN CHANG, Color and Shading Art Director

(this page) Deanna Marsigliese, *collage*

Deanna Marsigliese,
colored pencil and marker

Deanna Marsigliese, *ink and digital paint*

Enrico Casarosa, *colored pencil and watercolor*

19

Bolhem Bouchiba, *pencil*

(top row, middle)
Daniela Strijleva,
ink and digital paint

(everything else)
Deanna Marsigliese,
ink and digital paint

Deanna Marsigliese,
ink and digital paint

Greg Dykstra, *clay*

Jennifer Chia-Han Chang, *digital paint*

Tanja Krampfert, *digital sculpting*

Sea monster Luca is inspired by reef fish. Reef fish are very agile; they're elegant swimmers. This inspired Luca's round, soft shapes and fluid lines, not just throughout his body and fins, but in his posing and movement as well. We wanted to capture a very lyrical quality. —

DEANNA MARSIGLIESE, Character Art Director

(this page) Daniel López Muñoz,
pencil, marker, and digital paint

Enrico Casarosa,
pencil and watercolor

Deanna Marsigliese,
ink and digital paint

Daniela Strijleva,
ink and watercolor

Daniel López Muñoz, *pencil*

Deanna Marsigliese,
ink and digital paint

Deanna Marsigliese,
ink and digital paint

Deanna Marsigliese,
ink and digital paint

Greg Dykstra, *clay*

Jennifer Chia-Han Chang, *digital paint*

Trent Crow, *cloth shading*; Tanja Krampfert, *model/articulation*; Jacob Kuenzel, *eye shading*; Maria Lee, *skin shading*; Kiki Poh, *groom and hair shading*; Edgar Rodriguez, *tailoring*; Kevin Singleton, *articulation development*; Chuck Waite, *groom*

To bring the style and charm of Luca and Alberto's designs to life in three dimensions, the character artists collaborated with the designers to incorporate ideas from puppetry, 2D animation, stop motion, and sculpture. The final shapes, textures, and patterns were very deliberately constructed to create visual rhythm within the characters.

BETH ALBRIGHT, Character Supervisor

(this page) Deanna Marsigliese,
ink and digital paint

Deanna Marsigliese,
ink and digital paint

Jason Deamer, *pencil and digital paint*

We were inspired by scientific illustrations, hand-carved folk art, Japanese prints, and of course some of the earliest sea maps. All of these share a beautiful, ornate quality that reveals the hand of the artist. Similarly, we wanted our sea monsters to look like moving pieces of art—decoratively patterned and richly textured. Notice that as our sea monsters age, they grow more like the iconic sea monsters of those antique maps, with longer coiled tails and larger fins.

DEANNA MARSIGLIESE, Character Art Director

Deanna Marsigliese, *ink and digital paint*

(this page) Deanna Marsigliese,
ink, marker, and digital paint

32

Enrico Casarosa,
pencil and watercolor

The character artists worked closely with the designers to make sure every point, line, and curve was precisely placed and crafted for maximum appeal. Early digital sculpting was an excellent way to help Enrico figure out the proportions and appeal of the Paguro family in relation to Luca.

SAJAN SKARIA, Character Supervisor

Tanja Krampfert and Nancy Tsang,
digital sculpting

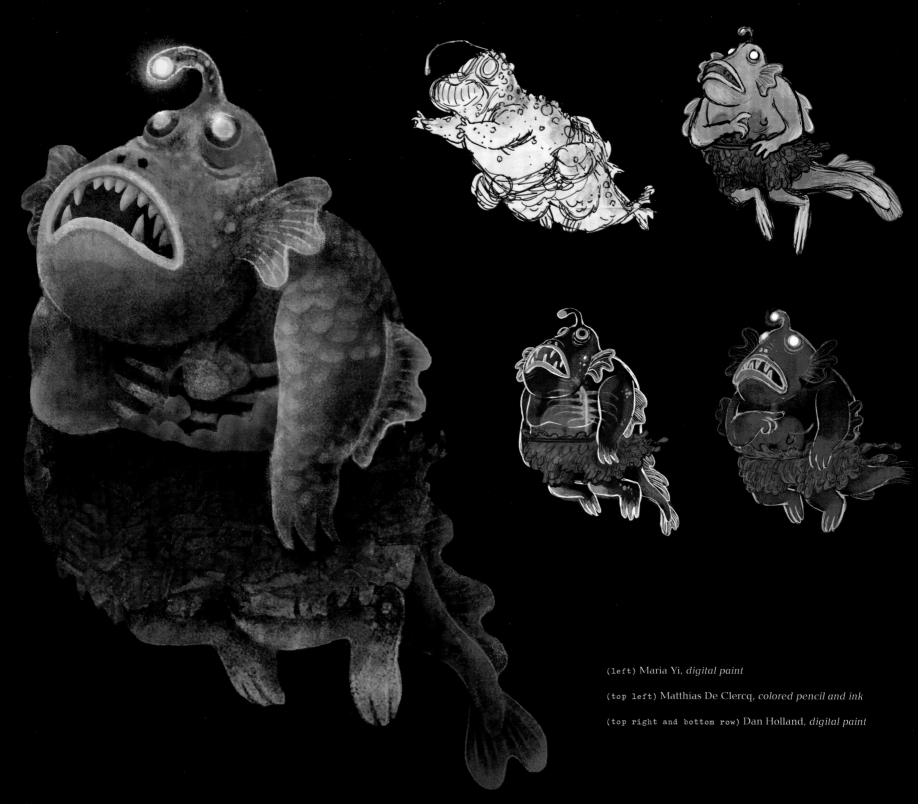

(left) Maria Yi, *digital paint*

(top left) Matthias De Clercq, *colored pencil and ink*

(top right and bottom row) Dan Holland, *digital paint*

Jamie Baker, Yon Hui Lee, and McKenna Harris, *digital storyboards*, "Busted"

Uncle Ugo represents the deep and Luca never getting to see his friend Alberto again. Becoming transparent isn't an attractive option either.

JOHN HOFFMAN, Story Supervisor

Deanna Marsigliese, *collage*

(above) Deanna Marsigliese, *ink and digital paint*

(left) Maria Yi, *pencil and digital paint*

37

(opposite) Josh West, *previs model*

(above) Don Shank, *digital paint*

For the design of the homes underwater, it was a balance to find something that reads like a home but isn't too human. At the same time, we were looking for something that felt ocean-like in its shaping. The design was based heavily on the Italian trullo house, which you find in the south of Italy in Puglia. They are dry-stacked houses that have a conical roof. They look like they are from nature, almost oceanic, as if they have scales.

DON SHANK, Sets Art Director

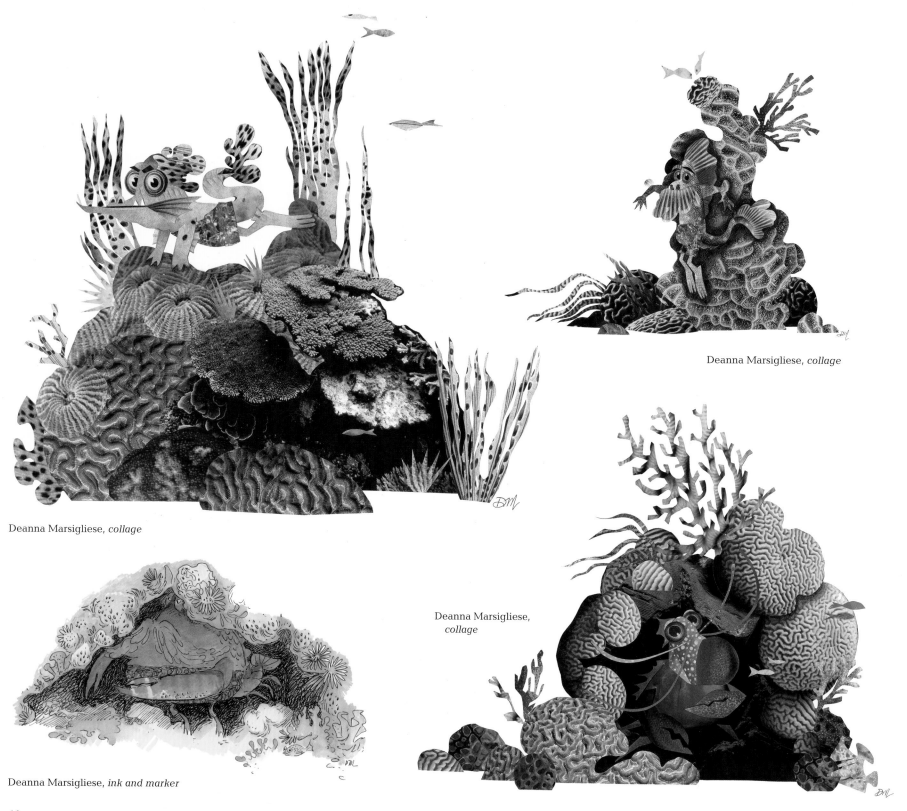

Deanna Marsigliese, *collage*

Deanna Marsigliese, *collage*

Deanna Marsigliese,
collage

Deanna Marsigliese, *ink and marker*

40

Deanna Marsigliese, *ink and marker*

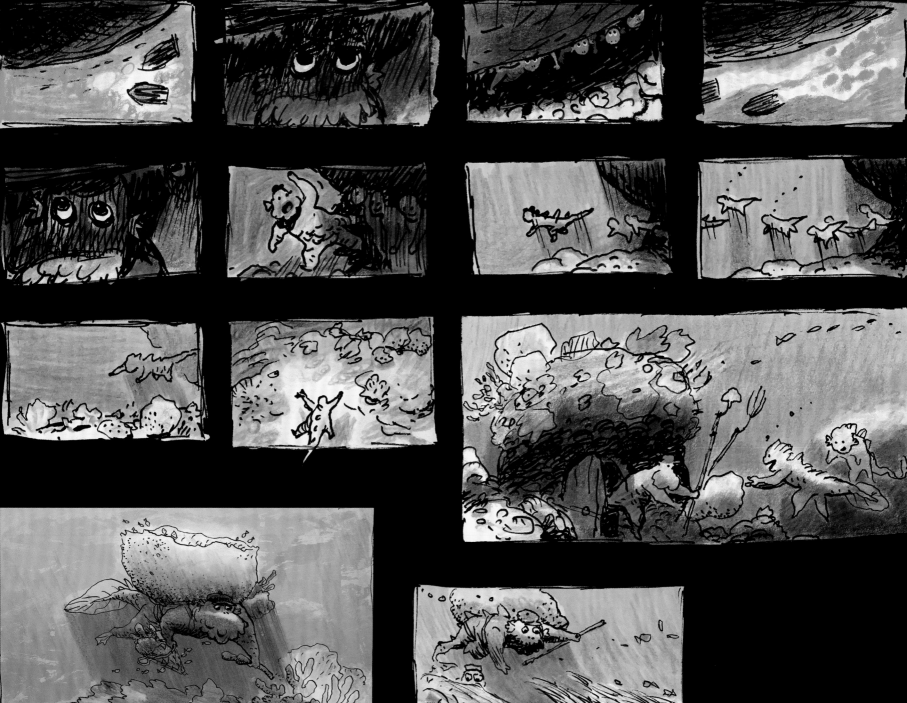

(this page) Daniel López Muñoz,
colored pencil and ink

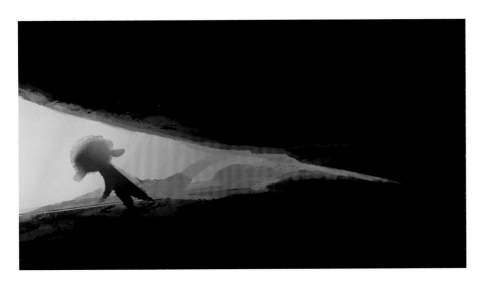

(this page) Daniela Strijleva, *digital paint*

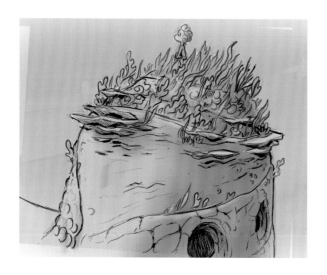

Nat McLaughlin, *digital paint*

Garrett Taylor, *digital paint*

Garrett Taylor, *digital paint*

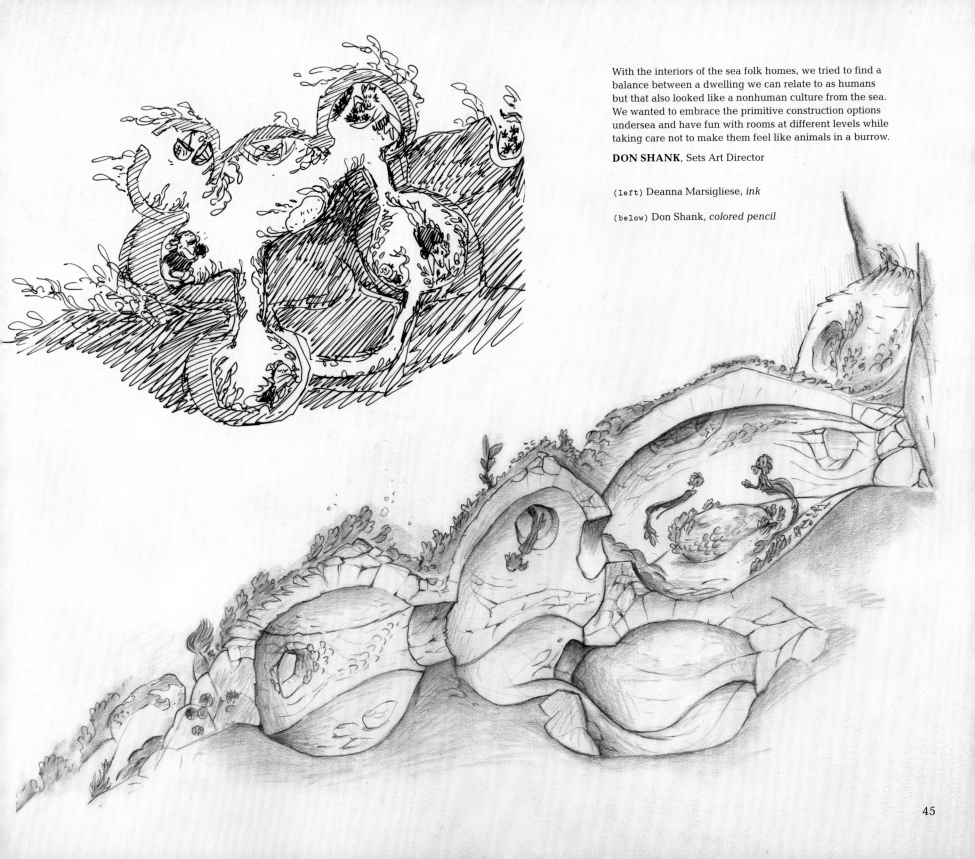

With the interiors of the sea folk homes, we tried to find a balance between a dwelling we can relate to as humans but that also looked like a nonhuman culture from the sea. We wanted to embrace the primitive construction options undersea and have fun with rooms at different levels while taking care not to make them feel like animals in a burrow.

DON SHANK, Sets Art Director

(left) Deanna Marsigliese, *ink*

(below) Don Shank, *colored pencil*

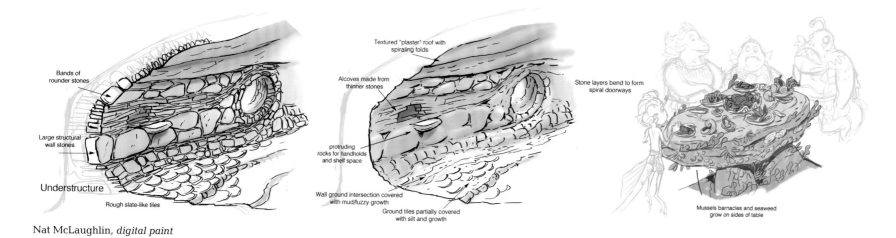

Bands of
rounder stones

Large structural
wall stones

Understructure

Rough slate-like tiles

Textured "plaster" roof with
spiraling folds

Alcoves made from
thinner stones

protruding
rocks for handholds
and shelf space

Wall ground intersection covered
with mud/fuzzy growth

Ground tiles partially covered
with silt and growth

Stone layers bend to form
spiral doorways

Mussels barnacles and seaweed
grow on sides of table

Nat McLaughlin, *digital paint*

Ernesto Nemesio, *digital paint*;
Gaston Ugarte, *modeling*

Sylvain Marc, *digital paint*

Daniel López Muñoz, *digital paint*

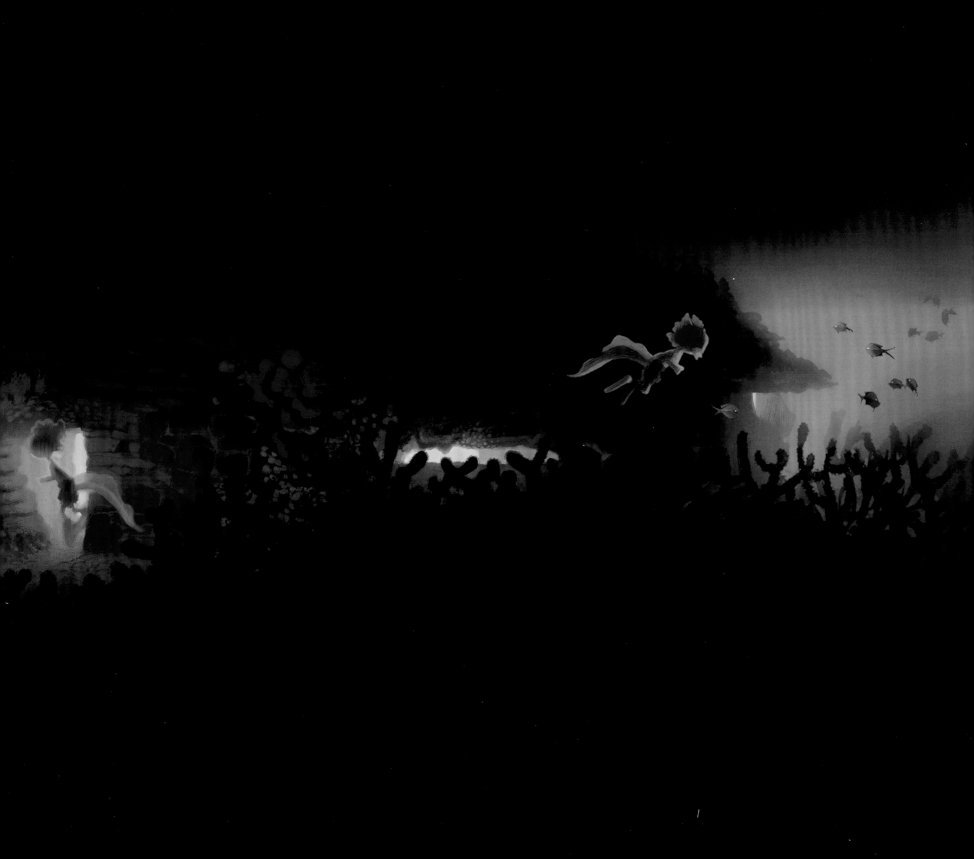

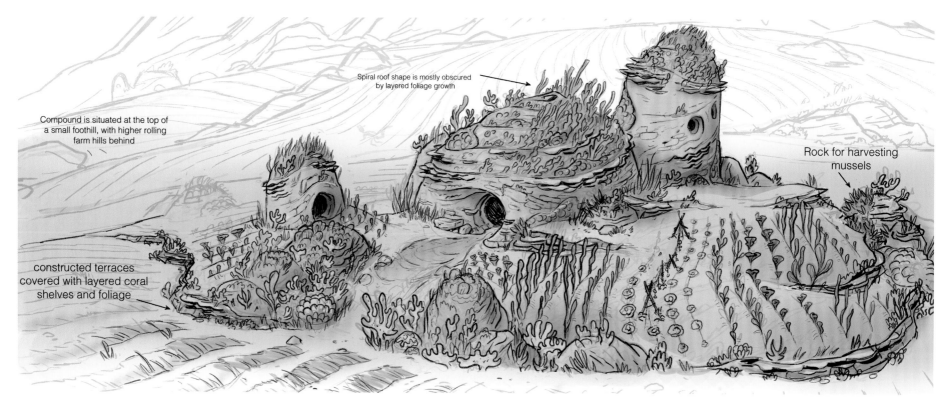

Spiral roof shape is mostly obscured by layered foliage growth

Compound is situated at the top of a small foothill, with higher rolling farm hills behind

Rock for harvesting mussels

constructed terraces covered with layered coral shelves and foliage

Nat McLaughlin, *digital paint*

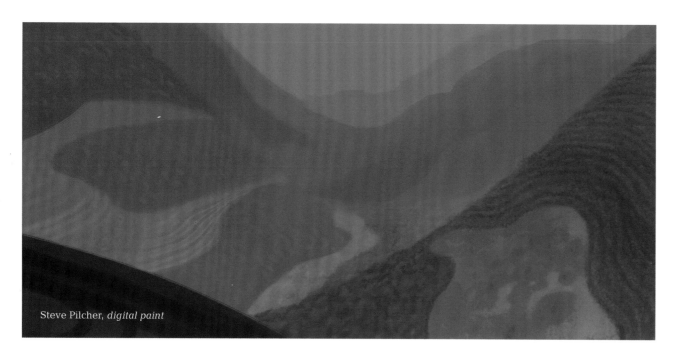

Steve Pilcher, *digital paint*

Deanna Marsigliese,
ink and digital paint

Underwater, the sea monsters are farmers living a hidden, quiet life. The visual language is horizontal, calm. There's a lot of murk, so you can't see very far. It's a soft, gently moving, sinuous world.

DANIELA STRIJLEVA, Production Designer

Daniel López Muñoz, *digital paint*

Daniel López Muñoz, *digital paint*

Daniel López Muñoz, *digital paint*

Kristian Norelius, *digital paint*

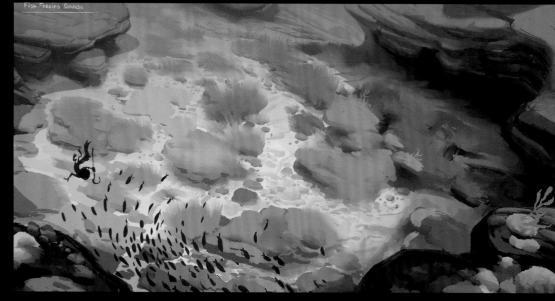

FISH FEEDING GROUNDS.

To contrast the human-made environments of the world above, we used rounded organic shapes and elegant sweeping curves to design the world underwater. The innate properties of water also guided us to skew our color palette cooler in temperature, and allowed for abstract, edgeless backdrops due to atmospheric perspective.

PAUL ABADILLA, Sets Art Director

Kristian Norelius, *digital paint*

Daniela Strijleva, *ink and digital paint*

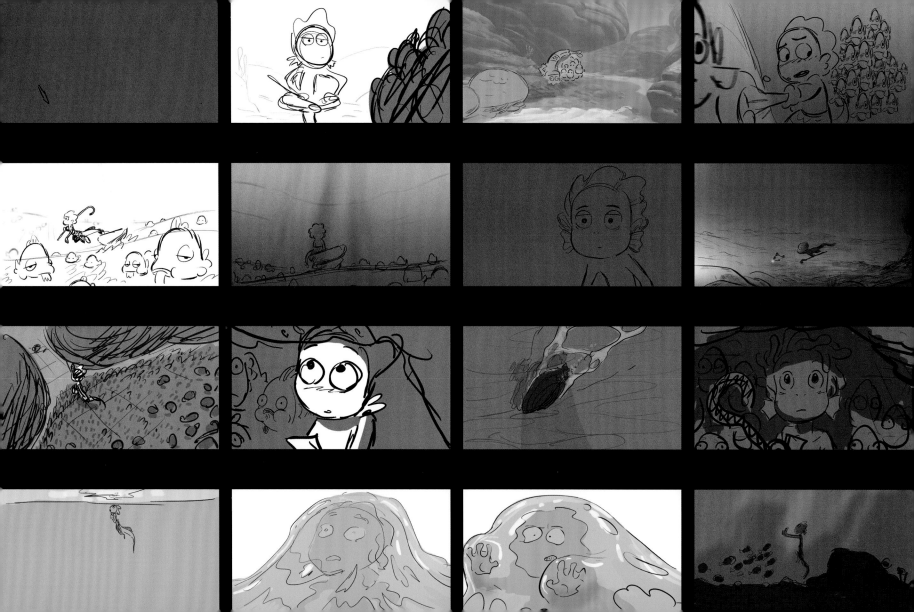

Nicolle Castro, Enrico Casarosa, and McKenna Harris, *digital storyboards*, "Family Lunch"

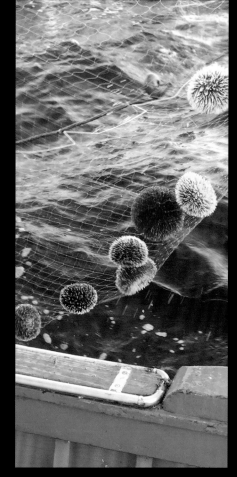

The beautiful aqua color of the water is such a brilliant feature of the Cinque Terre. We knew in lighting that it would be important for us to capture that lovely color and the overall appearance of the water to help give the movie that specificity of place.

KIM WHITE,
Director of Photography—Lighting

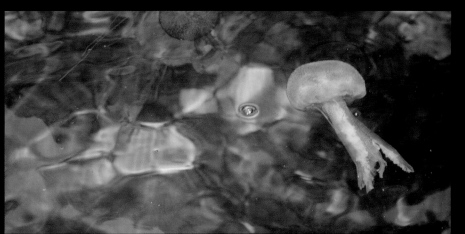

Harley Jessup, *photo collage*

Ernesto Nemesio, *digital paint*; Nick Pitera, *modeling*

ISLAND

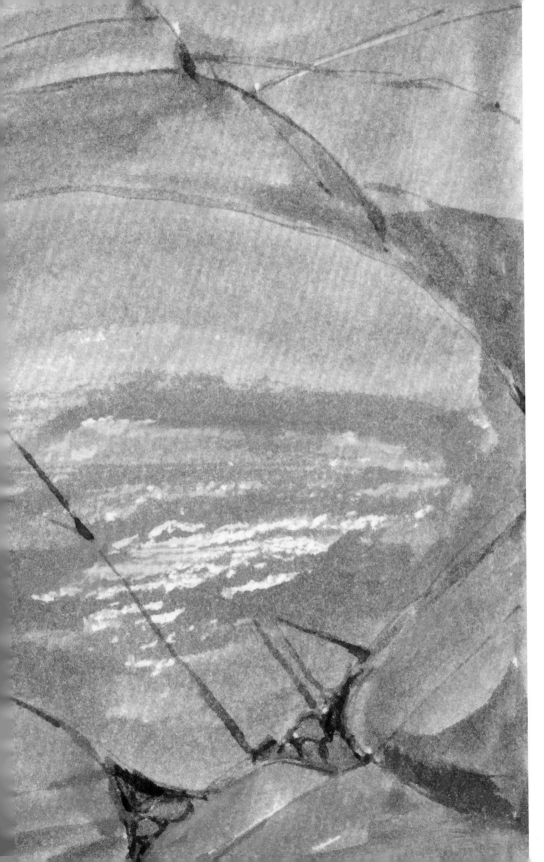

(above) Daniel López Muñoz, *digital paint*

(left) Daniela Strijleva, *gouache*

Deanna Marsigliese, *ink and digital paint*

We treated Alberto as an open water fish, like a swordfish or tuna—strong and powerful, with a silvery quality that camouflages well in open water. His design language has a sharper quality that aligns well with his personality. Note his spiky spines and sharp scallops. Unlike Luca, he's more of an erratic swimmer—impulsive and quick to change direction!

DEANNA MARSIGLIESE, Character Art Director

Tom Gately, *pencil*

Greg Dykstra, *clay*

Jennifer Chia-Han Chang and
Daniel López Muñoz, *digital paint*

Enrico Casarosa,
pencil and watercolor

Daniel López Muñoz, *ink*

Deanna Marsigliese,
ink and digital paint

Deanna Marsigliese,
ink and digital paint

Deanna Marsigliese, *ink and digital paint*

Deanna Marsigliese, *ink and digital paint*

Daniel López Muñoz, *colored pencil and marker*

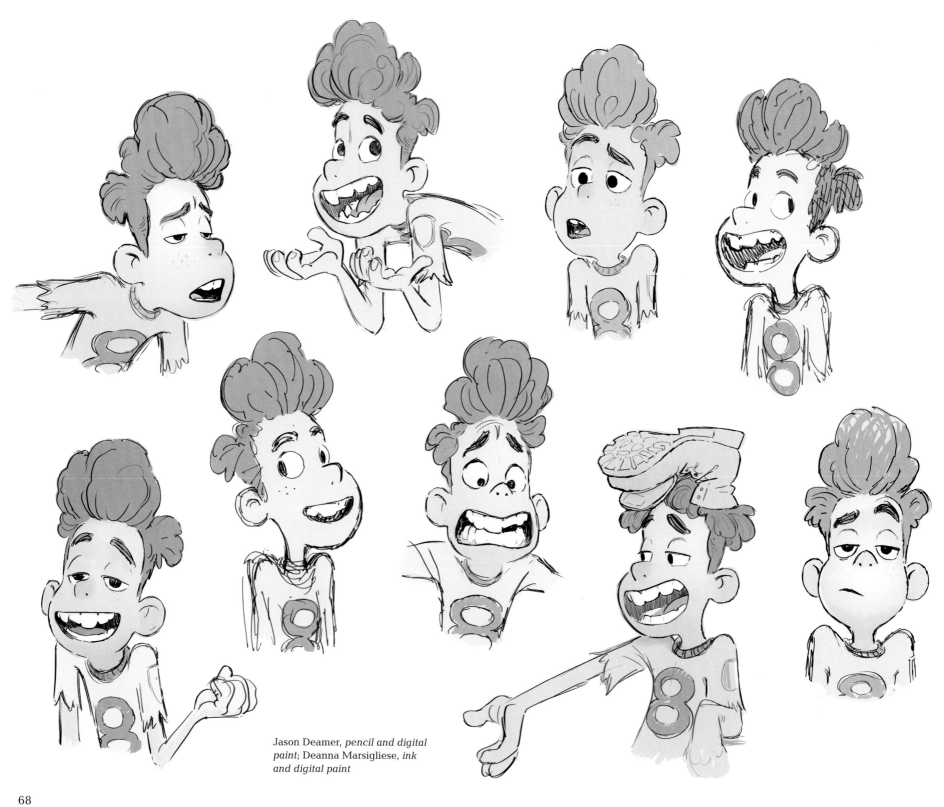

Jason Deamer, *pencil and digital paint*; Deanna Marsigliese, *ink and digital paint*

Greg Dykstra, *clay*

Jennifer Chia-Han Chang, *digital paint*

McKenna Harris,
digital paint

Mitra Shahidi,
digital paint

McKenna Harris,
digital paint

McKenna Harris,
digital paint

McKenna Harris, *ink*

Daniela Strijleva,
ink and watercolor

(this spread) Deanna Marsigliese, *ink and digital paint*

"DON'T WORRY— THIS SHIRT DIDN'T FIT ME VERY WELL EITHER". — ALBERTO

EATING LIKE "THEM"

73

Daniela Strijleva, *ink and digital paint*

(bottom row) Steve Pilcher, *digital paint*

74

Don Shank, *digital paint*

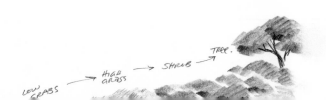

LOW GRASS → HIGH GRASS → SHRUB → TREE.

Josh West, Gaston Ugarte, and Nick Pitera, *modeling*;
Christina Garcia Weiland and Michael Rutter, *dressing*;
Andrew Finley and David Munier, *shading*

Daniel López Muñoz, *digital paint*

(above) Josh Holtsclaw, *digital*

(left) Kristian Norelius, *digital paint*

Josh Holtsclaw, *digital*

Laura Phillips, *digital paint*

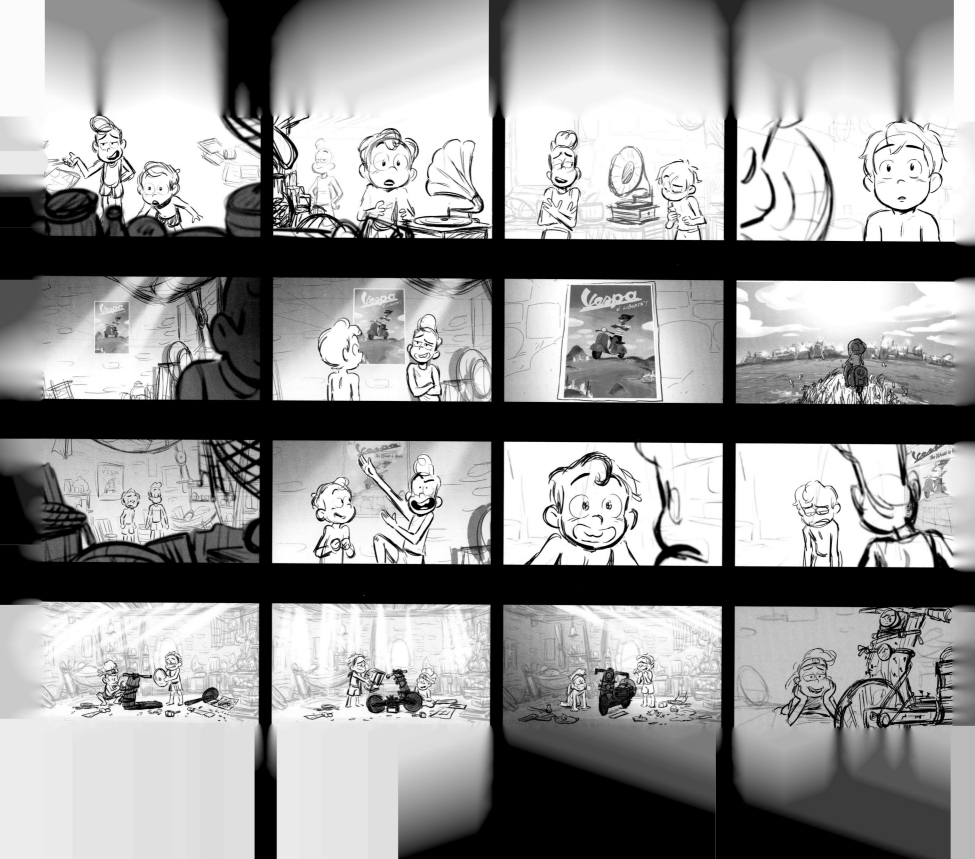

The Vespa Dream is the first time that Luca has a costar in one of his moments of fantasy: Alberto. It all starts with that poster, and it takes them all the way to the human world.

JOHN HOFFMAN, Story Supervisor

Lorenzo Fresta, *digital storyboards*, "Vespa Dream"

Lorenzo Fresta, *digital paint*

(this spread) Bill Cone, *pastels*

83

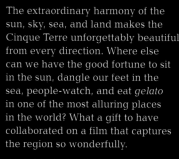

The extraordinary harmony of the sun, sky, sea, and land makes the Cinque Terre unforgettably beautiful from every direction. Where else can we have the good fortune to sit in the sun, dangle our feet in the sea, people-watch, and eat *gelato* in one of the most alluring places in the world? What a gift to have collaborated on a film that captures the region so wonderfully.

JAYME RODERICK,
Executive Assistant to the Producer

Harley Jessup, *photo collage*

Tadahiro Uesugi, *digital paint*

When Luca and Alberto get to Portorosso, they are amazed by the vibrant sounds and colors they see. The piazza is the heart of the town and full of activity. Every group of people they encounter tells a little story about the daily life of the townsfolk.

In real life, the Cinque Terre villages are small and everyone knows each other, and you observe so many little vignettes of daily life unfolding in front of you: Someone is singing at their window while hanging laundry; a group of elders chats at a bench; kids are always playing soccer somewhere that is not allowed. This is the slice-of-life quality that we wanted to capture.

DANIELA STRIJLEVA,
Production Designer

(opposite) Tadahiro Uesugi, *digital*

(right) Daniela Strijleva, *pencil, ink, and gouache*

Matthias De Clercq, *colored pencil and ink*

Enrico Casarosa,
pencil and watercolor

(above and left)
Daniela Strijleva,
ink and watercolor

(this page) Deanna Marsigliese,
ink and digital paint

(top row) Daniela Strijleva,
ink and watercolor

(bottom row) Deanna
Marsigliese, *ink and marker*

92

(this page) Deanna Marsigliese,
ink and marker

93

Deanna Marsigliese, *ink and digital paint*

Giulia is edgy, confident, and competitive, which is reflected in the triangular shapes of her design, right down to her pants. We like to imagine that these pants are hand-me-downs from Massimo's own childhood; a proud fisherman's daughter, she even shares Massimo's nose. Sharp, witty, focused, and direct, she leads with that beautiful nose.

DEANNA MARSIGLIESE, Character Art Director

Greg Dykstra, *clay*

Michael Nieves, *model and rig*;
Stacey Truman, *shading*; Ben Porter, *groom*

Jennifer Chia-Han Chang,
digital paint

95

Yon Hui Lee, *digital paint*

Wonderfully weird, passionate, and just, Giulia's the kind of friend I wish I had, and especially the friend I strive to be.

McKENNA HARRIS, Story Lead

LAUGH WITH ME! BWA HA HA HA HA HA

Sorry, sweaty planner

gets too into stuff/ starts sweating

12 year old me

ponytail = serious giulia being really freakin' serious

TAP TAP TAP

YOU KNOW WHAT TASTES BETTER THAN SPAGHETTI? VICTORY.

McKenna Harris, *digital paint*

Giulia wields FISH in the way King Arthur wielded EXCALIBUR.

BASTA ERCOLE. DON'T MAKE ME USE THIS.

ALT: I CAN AND WILL SLAP YOU WITH A FISH.

McKenna Harris, *digital paint*

Daniela Strijleva, *ink and digital paint*

McKenna Harris, *digital paint*

Bolhem Bouchiba, *pencil*

Nicolle Castro, *digital paint*

McKenna Harris, *digital paint*

(above and below)
Deanna Marsigliese,
marker and digital paint

Chris Sasaki, *digital paint*

100

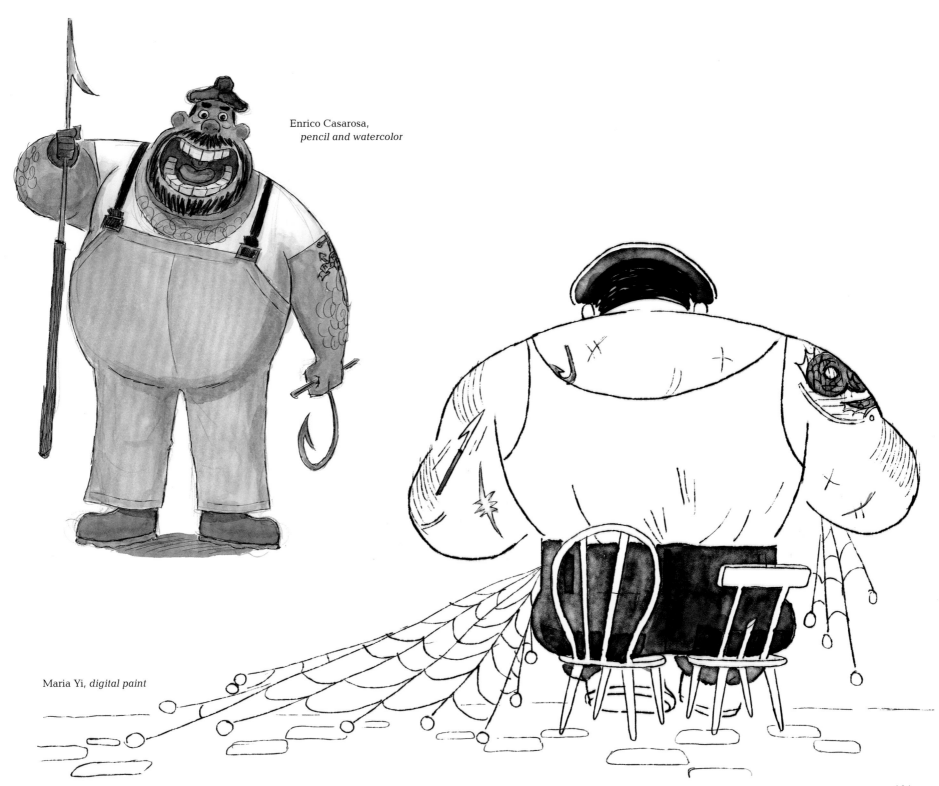

Enrico Casarosa, *pencil and watercolor*

Maria Yi, *digital paint*

Maria Yi, *digital paint*

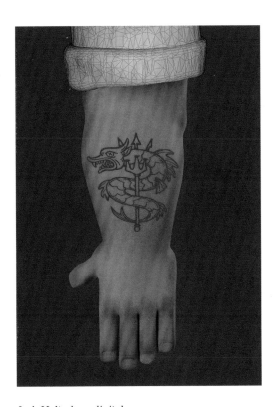

Josh Holtsclaw, *digital*

Maria Yi, *digital paint*

Laura Phillips, *digital paint*

103

Maria Yi,
digital paint

Deanna Marsigliese,
ink and digital paint

Nicolle Castro, *ink*

104

Maria Yi, *digital paint*

(above and below) Maria Yi, *digital paint*

HANG IN THERE

Nicolle Castro, *digital paint*

105

Dan Holland, *pencil*

Jason Deamer, *pencil and digital paint*

Dan Holland, *colored pencil and ink*

Jason Deamer, *pencil and digital paint*

Deanna Marsigliese, *pencil and digital paint*

106

Maria Yi, *digital paint*

Brian Kalin O'Connell, *digital storyboards,* "Cove Red"

(this page) Deanna Marsigliese,
ink and marker

(opposite) Deanna Marsigliese,
ink and digital paint

(above) Deanna Marsigliese, *pencil and digital paint*

(left and below) Tom Gately, *pencil*

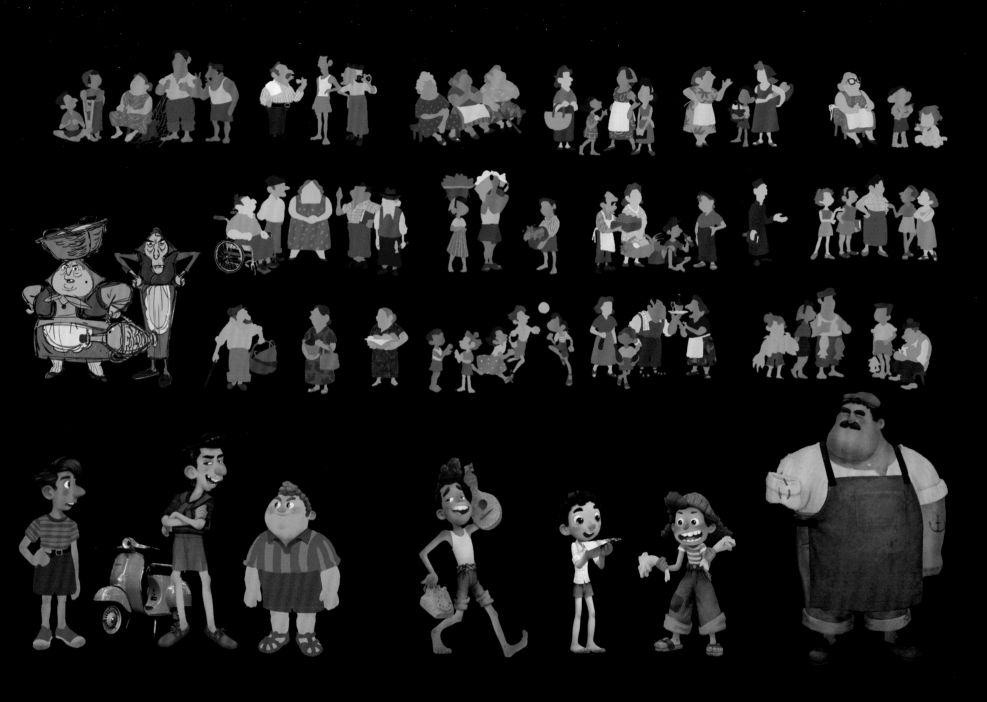

Daniela Strijleva, Deanna Marsigliese,
Maria Yi, Laura Phillips, and Jennifer
Chia-Han Chang, *digital paint*

We approached the color palette of the townsfolk with the same spirit as the color palette
for the town buildings. Both elements are very much a part of the storybook-like world, so
we kept the color palette rich and warm. That way, the townsfolk and environment create a
setting saturated in color, which surrounds and contrasts against the simpler main characters.
The warm and earthy color palette also balances the cooler colors of the underwater world.

JENNIFER CHIA-HAN CHANG, Color and Shading Art Director

(this spread)
Deanna Marsigliese,
ink and digital paint

113

Daniela Strijleva, *pencil and gouache*

114

Noah Klocek,
pencil and digital paint

Don Shank, *digital paint*

115

Enrico Casarosa, *pencil*

(above) Josh West, *previs model, modeling, shading, and lighting*

(left) Daniela Strijleva, *digital paint*

Don Shank, *pencil*

Don Shank, *colored pencil and ink*

Ernesto Nemesio, *digital paint*

To capture the look and feel of a story told through a kid's eyes, we were inspired by storybooks, theatrical plays, and impressionist paintings. We tried to distill the clues and elements of a place and time to maximize the expression of storytelling.

JENNIFER CHIA-HAN CHANG,
Color and Shading Art Director

Our piazza is designed with three sides of buildings opening up to the sea, like a theater set. We wanted our town to have that same artisan quality you see in practical sets. To achieve that, we reduced the number of architectural elements needed on a building, grouped them deliberately, exaggerated the scale of doors, windows, and laundry, and as much as possible we let the beautiful texture of the walls tell the rest of the story. We distilled the storytelling to its main components and moved away from realism.

DANIELA STRIJLEVA,
Production Designer

Tadahiro Uesugi, *ink and digital paint*

In Portorosso, everything is vertical. If underwater, things are sinuous and horizontal, the town, by contrast, has hard surfaces and vertical buildings. The Cinque Terre towns that we were inspired by are very unique. They are perched on these steep hills between the mountains and the sea; over the centuries, people built their houses on impossible ridges. The streets are very, very narrow, with meandering staircases between them.

DANIELA STRIJLEVA, Production Designer

(opposite and below) Don Shank, *pencil on paper, wire, tape, hot glue, and photography*

(top row) Don Shank, *colored pencil and ink*

Daniela Strijleva and Daniel López Muñoz, *digital paint*; Don Shank, *paper model*

Jennifer Chia-Han Chang, *digital paint*

Josh Holtsclaw, *digital*

Josh West, *modeling*; Andrew Finley, Jack Hatori, and Mallory Kohut, *shading*; Michael Rutter, *dressing*; Josh Holtsclaw, *graphics design*; Rich Snyder, *graphics installation*

We wanted to take some of the charm and the expressive quality of a miniature, the reductive quality of it, but not throw away the very thin and elegant features, making it like a miniature on a human scale.

DON SHANK, Sets Art Director

123

ALIMENTARI
REPETTO

VIA
STELLINA

19

PREZZI
ONESTI

PRODOTTI TIPICI

CARNE
BOVINA E SUINA

PANE
FRESCO

PANINI
RIPIENI

OTTIMA QUALITÀ

FRUTTA
VERDURA

UN PO
DI
TUTTO

5⁹⁵

2⁹⁵

5

2⁹⁵

⁹⁵

2⁹⁵

The graphic design found throughout the towns of coastal Italy is incredibly inspiring. It paints a detailed picture of the history of the region and the people who live there. For *Luca*, we wanted our designs to feel like they had a history of their own, and we wanted to help tell the story of the characters that live in Portorosso. We took the inspiration from our research and combined it with a handcrafted, childlike design aesthetic to find a graphic look that hopefully fits seamlessly into the environments of our film and into the lives of our characters.

JOSH HOLTSCLAW, Graphics Art Director

(top row) Josh Holtsclaw, *digital paint*

Josh Holtsclaw, *ink and digital*

Bert Berry, *digital paint*

BY YON + MATTHIAS
TOOLS SUPPORT BY MATTHIAS, STEPHAN + JOSHUA

BY YON + MATTHIAS
TOOLS SUPPORT BY MATTHIAS, STEPHAN + JOSHUA

(opposite) Matthias De Clercq (layout)
and Yon Hui Lee (final art), *digital paint*

(this page) Tadahiro Uesugi, *digital paint*

Jennifer Chia-Han Chang, *digital paint*

Marcovaldo Pescheria

Don Shank, *pencil*

130

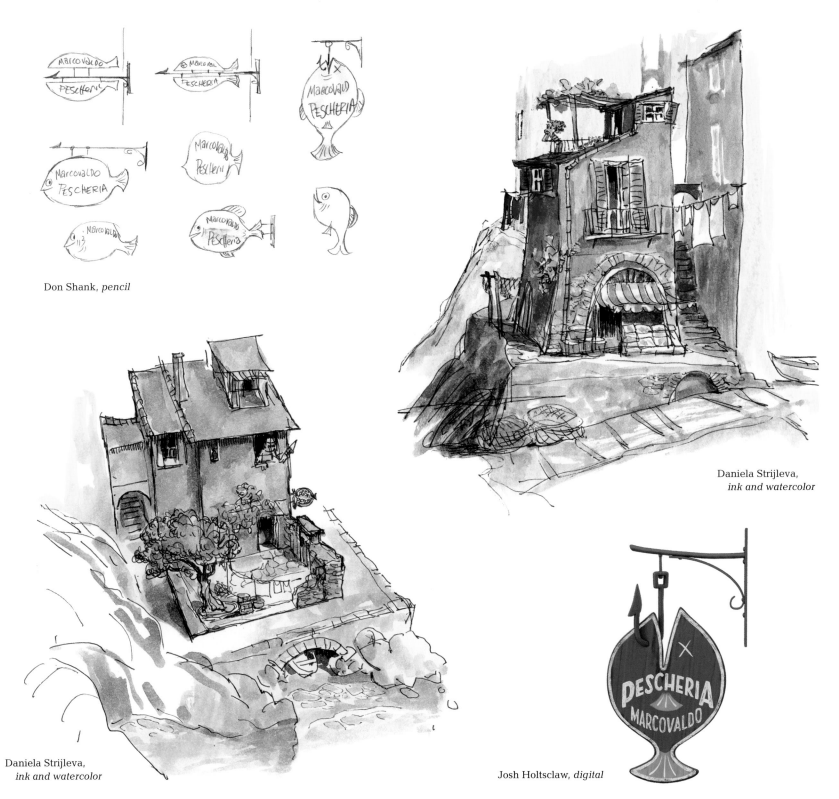

Don Shank, *pencil*

Daniela Strijleva,
ink and watercolor

Daniela Strijleva,
ink and watercolor

Josh Holtsclaw, *digital*

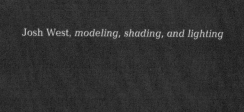

132

Josh West, *modeling*; Tracy Lee Church, *shading*; Michael Rutter, *dressing*

Jennifer Chia-Han Chang and Ernesto Nemesio, *digital paint*

133

Daniela Strijleva, *ink*

Don Shank, *pencil*

Paul Abadilla and Jennifer Chia-Han Chang, *digital paint*

134

Daniela Strijleva, *digital paint*

Maria Yi, *digital paint*

Josh Holtsclaw, *digital*

Daniel López Muñoz, *pencil*

Josh Holtsclaw, *digital*

McKenna Harris, *digital paint*

Chris Sasaki, *digital paint*

137

Daniela Strijleva, *ink*

Bert Berry, *digital*

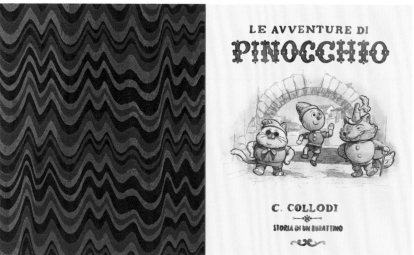

(bottom row) Josh Holtsclaw, *ink and digital*

138

Daniel López Muñoz, *digital*; Tracy Lee Church, *shading*;
Nick Pitera, *modeling and dressing*

(above) Daniela Strijleva and Laura Phillips,
digital paint; Josh West, *render*

(opposite) Daniel López Muñoz, *digital paint*

141

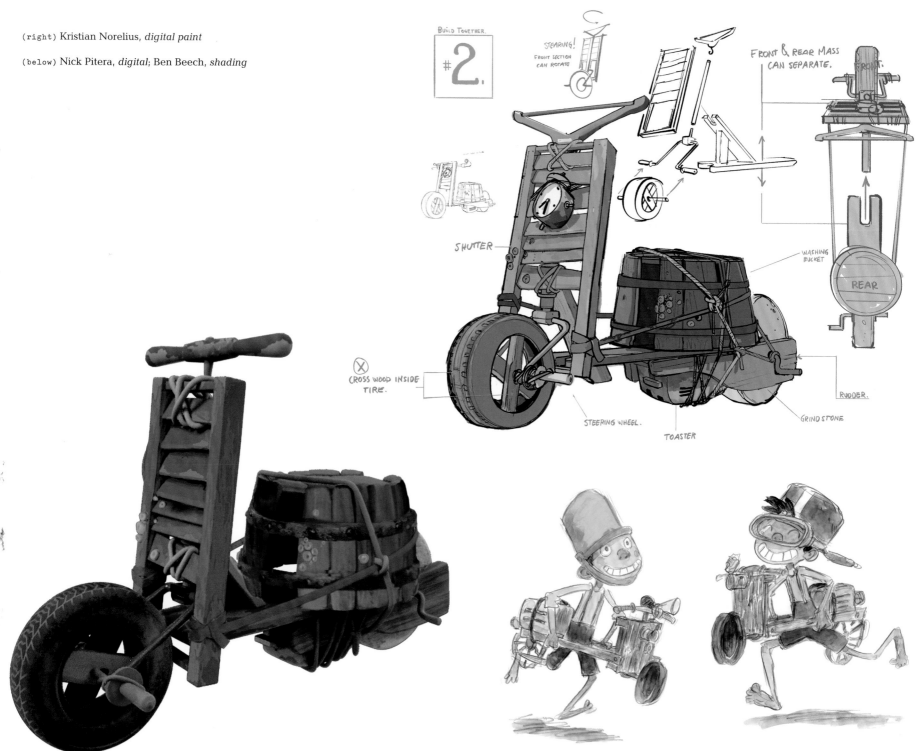

(right) Kristian Norelius, *digital paint*

(below) Nick Pitera, *digital*; Ben Beech, *shading*

BUILD TOGETHER.
2.

STEARING!
FRONT SECTION CAN ROTATE

FRONT & REAR MASS CAN SEPARATE.

FRONT.

SHUTTER

WASHING BUCKET

REAR

CROSS WOOD INSIDE TIRE.

STEERING WHEEL.

TOASTER

RUDDER.

GRINDSTONE

Enrico Casarosa, *pencil and watercolor*

1950 Vespa 125

OLD-Vespa

BACK SEAT. | FRONT SEAT

SAME MODEL AS OLD VESPA

FRONT LIGHT.

KICK.

Kristian Norelius, *digital paint*

RIPARAZIONI

MECCANICO

27

EXTENDED BACK WALL.

(above) Laura Phillips, *digital*; Josh Holtsclaw, *graphics*

(left) Kristian Norelius, *digital*; Josh Holtsclaw, *graphics*

143

Louise Smythe, Scott Morse, and Lorenzo Fresta, *digital storyboards*, "Wipeout"

(this page) Kristian Norelius,
digital paint

145

ERCOLE Bike
·Variant·

Luca/Giulia Bike ·Variant·

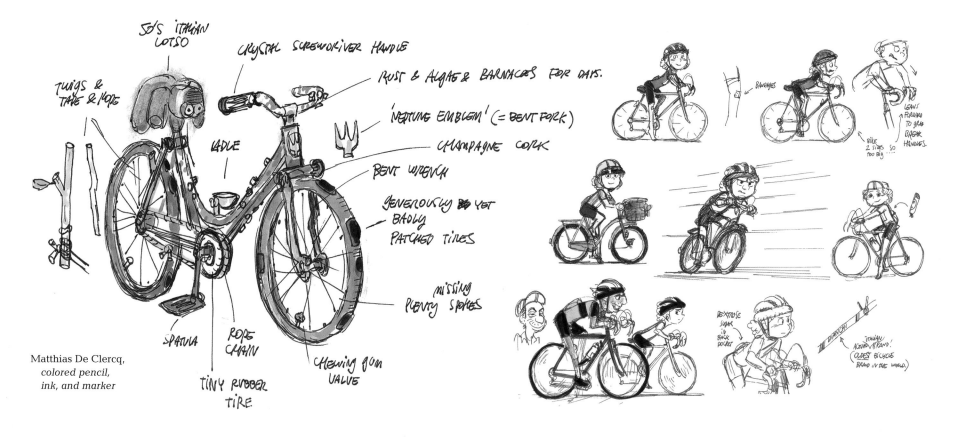

50'S ITALIAN
LOTSO

TWIGS &
TAPE & HOPE

CRYSTAL SCREWDRIVER HANDLE

RUST & ALGAE & BARNACLES FOR DAYS.

'NEPTUNE EMBLEM' (= BENT FORK)

LADLE

CHAMPAGNE CORK

BENT WRENCH

GENEROUSLY yet
BADLY
PATCHED TIRES

missing
PLENTY SPOKES

SPATULA

ROPE
CHAIN

CHEWING GUM
VALVE

TINY RUBBER
TIRE

Matthias De Clercq,
*colored pencil,
ink, and marker*

BANDAGES

LEANS
FORWARD
TO GRAB
BRAKE
HANDLES.

BIKE
2 SIZES SO
TOO BIG ....

DEXTROSE
SUGAR
IN BACK
POCKET

ITALIAN
ACTUAL BRAND!
(OLDEST BICYCLE
BRAND IN THE WORLD.)

Bill Cone, *digital paint*

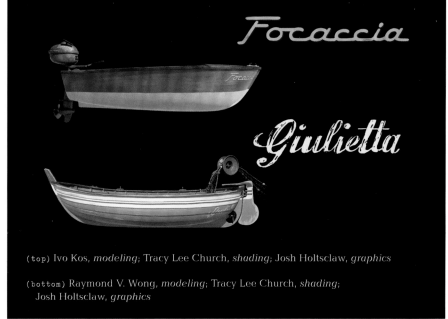

Focaccia

Giulietta

(top) Ivo Kos, *modeling*; Tracy Lee Church, *shading*; Josh Holtsclaw, *graphics*

(bottom) Raymond V. Wong, *modeling*; Tracy Lee Church, *shading*; Josh Holtsclaw, *graphics*

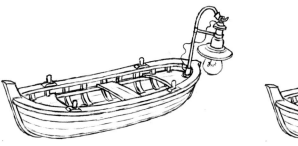

Nat McLaughlin, *digital paint*

Paul Conrad, *digital paint*

McKenna Harris, Nicolle Castro, Mitra Shahidi,
Matthias De Clercq, *digital storyboards*, "Without Alberto"

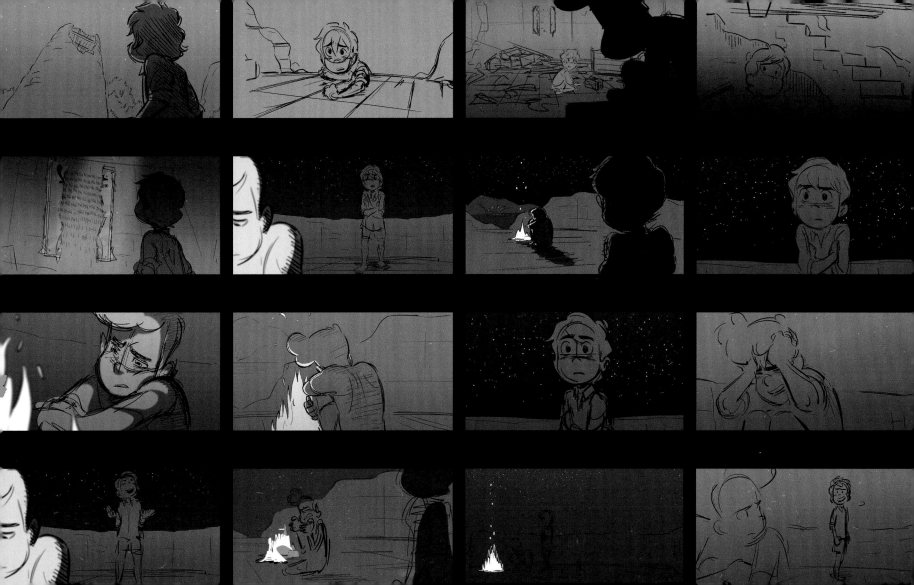

Jamie Baker, Yon Hui Lee, and Lorenzo Fresta, *digital storyboards*, "Finish Line"

Matthias De Clercq and McKenna Harris, *digital storyboards*, "Parting Ways"

When walking the streets of the Cinque Terre towns, we were quickly confronted with the verticality and irregularity of it all. You would start at sea level, enter an alley and take a few switchback sets of stairs, then suddenly pop out to a sunny exposed promontory overlooking the whole town. Using these dark and light spaces to craft compositions to frame our characters was a great way to capture the place.

DAVID JUAN BIANCHI,
Director of Photography

Harley Jessup, *photo collage*

(this spread) Ernesto Nemesio, Daniel López Muñoz, Paul Abadilla, and Jennifer Chia-Han Chang, *digital paint*

Think back on that one blue summer. We can all remember that one amazing childhood summer, marked by memories of the fearless friends with whom we experienced our passage into maturity. It was filled with splendid adventures in the summer sun and (if you were lucky enough) the sea. In painting the colorscripts, we endeavored to recapture those remote, indelible imprints on our young hearts. Joy, sadness, fear, hope—the Mediterranean summer sun offered a unique and honest warmth and vitality of color that is ultimately central to the themes we wanted to convey.

DANIEL LÓPEZ MUÑOZ, Color Script Artist

OUT OF PICTURE

Daniel López Muñoz, *digital paint*

We explore a lot of ideas on these films and travel down a lot of roads. Sometimes those roads show us exactly what we're looking for, and sometimes they're a dead end, but we always learn from them. Here is some exploratory artwork and storyboards from moments that may not have made it into the film, but they helped us find our way to what you saw up on the screen.

JOHN HOFFMAN, Story Supervisor

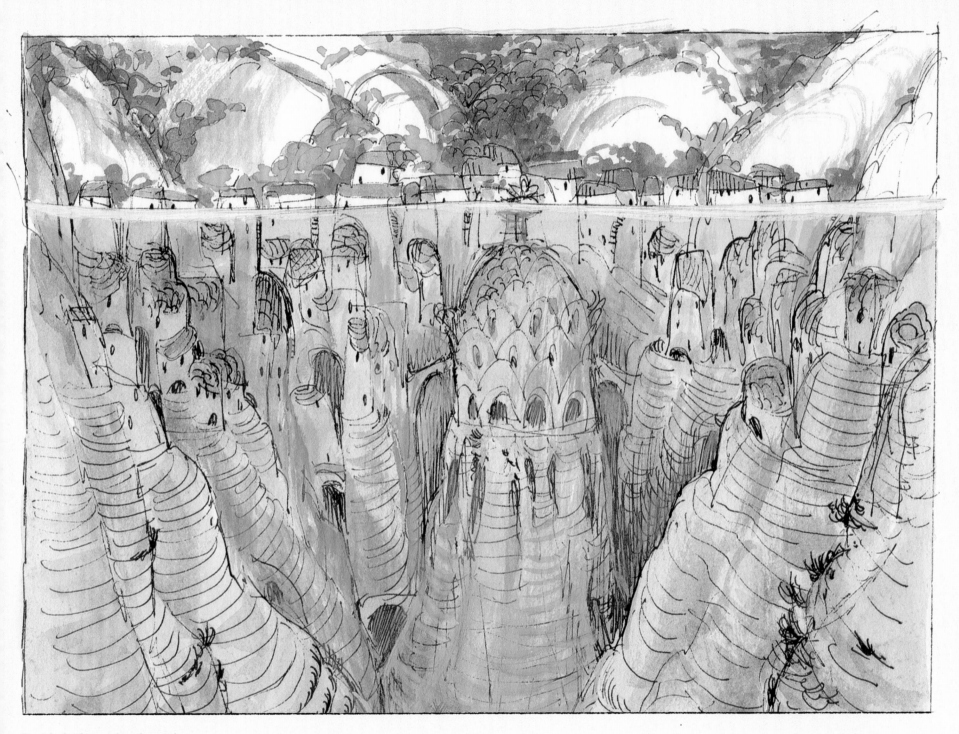

Daniela Strijleva, *ink and gouache*

(left) Vladimir Kooperman, *pencil*; Enrico Casarosa, *watercolor*

(below, right, and opposite) Enrico Casarosa, *pencil and watercolor*

Daniel López Muñoz, *colored pencil*

(above) Daniel López Muñoz, *ink and digital paint*

(right) Daniel López Muñoz, *colored pencil*

162

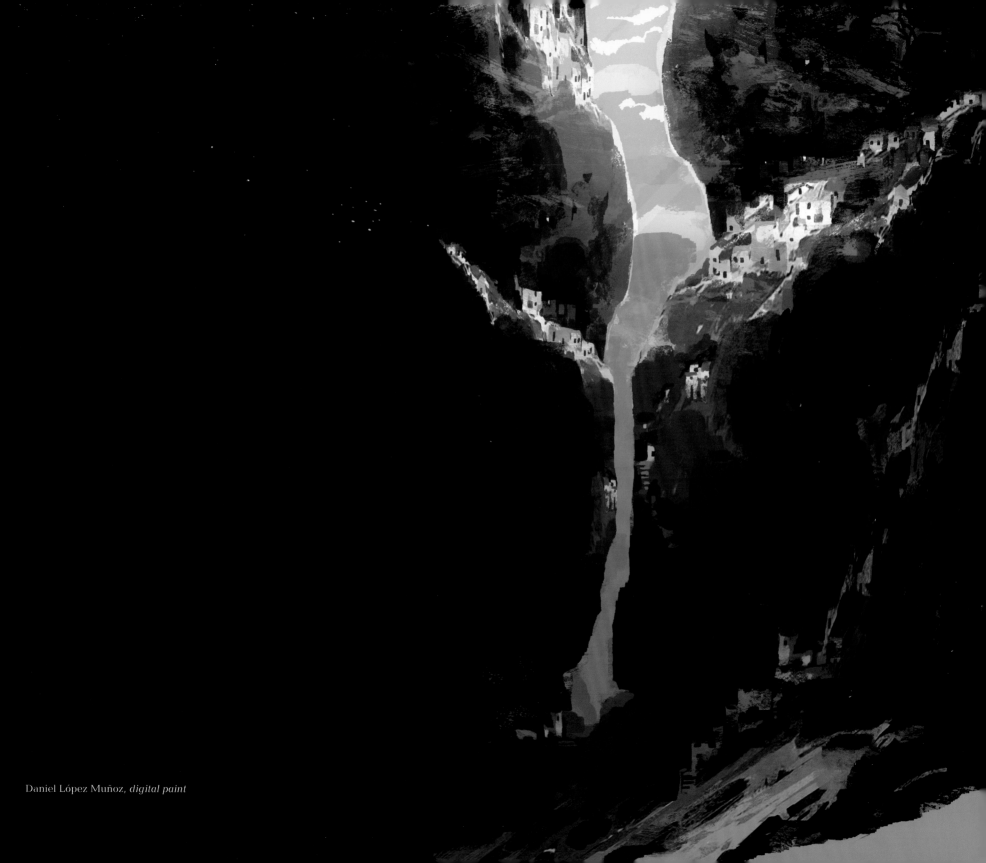

Daniel López Muñoz, *digital paint*

Enrico Casarosa, *pencil and watercolor*

McKenna Harris, *digital paint*

Daniela Strijleva, *digital paint*

Daniel López Muñoz, *digital paint*

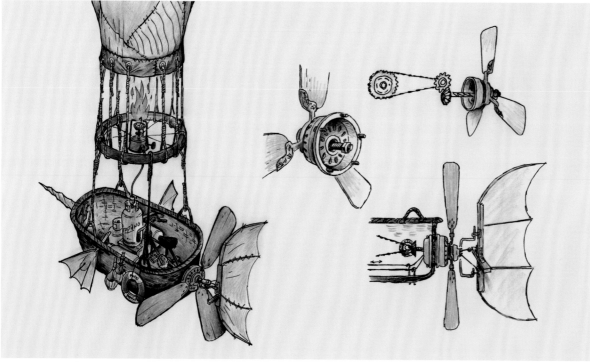

Don Shank, *colored pencil and ink*

Jennifer Chia-Han Chang, *digital paint*

166

Daniela Strijleva, *digital paint*

Daniela Strijleva, *digital paint*

(above and left) Sylvain Marc, *digital paint*

John Hoffman and Bolhem Bouchiba, *digital storyboards*, "I Can Walk"

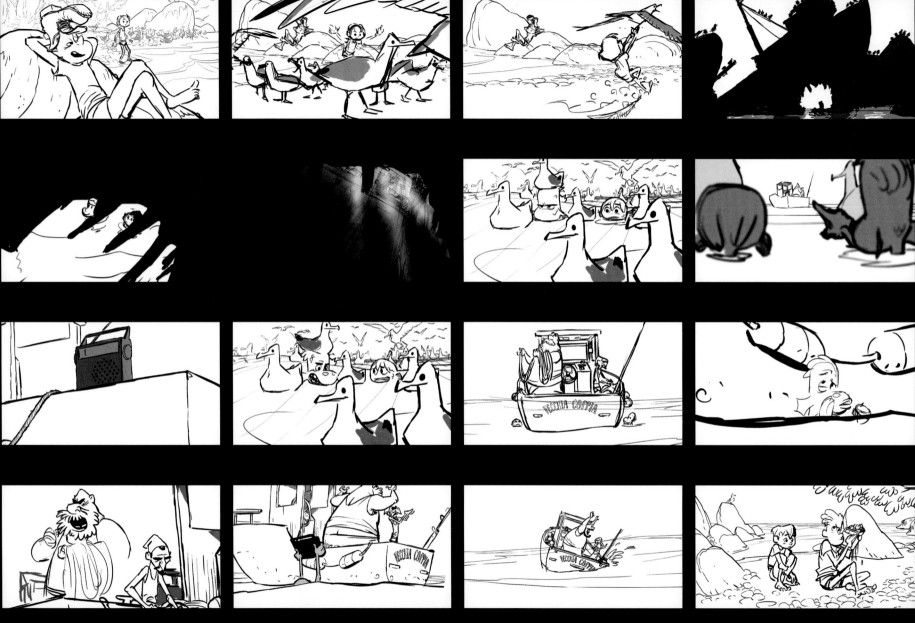

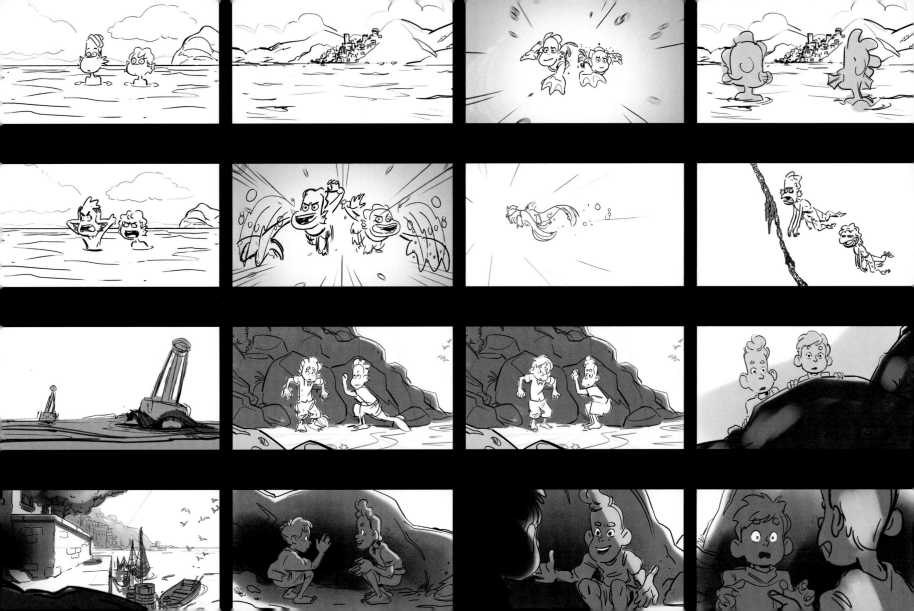

Xavier Riffault, *digital storyboards*, "Making the Rounds"

James Robertson, *digital storyboards*, "Daddy Issues"

ACKNOWLEDGMENTS

Enrico is a remarkable artist on multiple fronts—both poet and painter, gifted at reminding us all to see the meaning and beauty that exist all around us. Every day I am inspired not only by his creativity, but also by his character: hardworking, humble, and kind. *Grazie di avermi portata in questo viaggio straordinario!*

Thank you to *Luca*'s immensely talented Production Designer, Daniela Strijleva, for creating a breathtaking world that feels both magical and real enough to visit, so immersive we can practically taste the *gelato*! Dani was joined by Art Directors Deanna Marsigliese, Jennifer Chia-Han Chang, Don Shank, Josh Holtsclaw, and Paul Abadilla. Together they crafted the charming and unique style of the film, working with an accomplished team of artists: Daniel López Muñoz, Kristian Norelius, Ernesto Nemesio, Josh West, Noah Klocek, Nat McLaughlin, Philip Metschan, Maria Yi, Dan Holland, Jason Deamer, Greg Dykstra, Tanja Krampfert, Nancy Tsang, Laura Phillips, Bert Berry, Bill Cone, Harley Jessup, and Bolhem Bouchiba.

Neither this book nor the film itself would be possible without the astute leadership of the Art Department production team: Hana Yoon, Gerisa Macale, Deb Poznansky, and Paige Johnstone.

Thank you to Story Supervisor John Hoffman, who always impresses with his prolific, thoughtful outpouring of story ideas. Thank you also to Story Lead McKenna Harris, who brought such sweetness and life to each character. No matter how complicated the storytelling puzzle, the passion of *Luca*'s dedicated story team was unparalleled. A heartfelt thank you to Jamie Baker, Max Brace, Nicolle Castro, Koko Chou, Mike Daley, Matthias De Clercq, Lorenzo Fresta, Yon Hui Lee, Brian Kalin O'Connell, Mitra Shahidi, Louise Smythe, Xavier Riffault, James Robertson, and Nate Stanton.

Thank you to writers Jesse Andrews and Mike Jones for their unflagging investment in every detail of this story.

Thank you to Matt DeMartini, Jaclyn Grubin, and Mattie Brehm for seamlessly navigating the ever-winding path of story production and for contributing story ideas and production insights along the way.

We are grateful to the teams at Pixar and Chronicle Books, not only for making it possible to share this beautiful art with the world, but, in this case, for persevering through such challenging work-from-home circumstances. Thank you to Jenny Moussa Spring, Molly Jones, Deborah Cichocki, Shiho Tilley, Maura Turner, Melissa Bernabei, Kelsey Pighin, Liam Flanagan, Neil Egan, Julia Patrick, Alison Petersen, and Tera Killip for keeping it all moving forward. And thanks to Serena Dettman and Jini Chatterjee for always keeping us out of trouble.

We appreciate the many enlightening conversations we had with all of our consultants, who helped us make the film more authentic. Thank you to the executives at Pixar for their guidance along an uphill journey: Jim Morris, Jonas Rivera, Pete Docter, Katherine Sarafian, Tom Porter, Andrew Stanton, Steve May, Jim Kennedy, Britta Wilson, Chris Kaiser, Lindsey Collins, Jonathan Garson, and Reema Batnagar.

We are indebted to our Executive Producers, Peter Sohn and Kiri Hart, for their belief in the project, their wisdom, and their friendship. And thank you to our Associate Executive Producer, Carrie Hobson, for always contributing a fresh perspective and new ideas.

Leading the charge was a team overflowing with smarts, empathy, and a collaborative spirit: Will Reusch, Krissy Cababa, David Ryu, Jayme Roderick, and Kelley Losik. Thank you for all of the laughter and learning and for always finding a way to make the impossible possible.

It's hard enough to make a film under normal circumstances, but doing so during a global health crisis is exponentially more difficult. And yet, every day the crew made it happen, despite facing so many unprecedented challenges. I am amazed and humbled to have worked with this resilient, creative, committed group of filmmakers. *Grazie di tutto!*

Andrea Warren, Producer

(above) Maria Yi and Daniela Strijleva, *ink and digital paint*

(following page) Vladimir Kooperman and Enrico Casarosa, *pencil and watercolor*

Vespa

We train our
mechanics in
engines & style